NEW YORK REVIEW BOOKS

POETS

ELIZABETH WILLIS is the author of *Address* (2011), which received the PEN New England/L. L. Winship Prize, and four previous books of poetry. Her second book, *The Human Abstract* (1995), was selected for the National Poetry Series. A recent Guggenheim fellow in poetry, she teaches at Wesleyan University.

Elizabeth Willis

Alive
New and Selected Poems

NYRB/POETS

nyrb   NEW YORK REVIEW BOOKS   *New York*

THIS IS A NEW YORK REVIEW BOOK
PUBLISHED BY THE NEW YORK REVIEW OF BOOKS
435 Hudson Street, New York, NY 10014
www.nyrb.com

The Publisher would like to thank Wesleyan University Press for
permission to reprint poems from *Meteoric Flowers* and *Address*, and
Burning Deck Press for permission to reprint poems from *Turneresque*.

Library of Congress Cataloging-in-Publication Data
Willis, Elizabeth.
[Poems. Selections]
Alive : new and selected poems / Elizabeth Willis.
    pages ; cm. — (New York Review Books Poets)
ISBN 978-1-59017-864-5 (softcover)
I. Title.
PS3573.I456523A6 2015
811'.54—dc23

                    2014043162

ISBN 978-1-59017-864-5
Available as an electronic book; ISBN 978-1-59017-865-2

Cover and book design by Emily Singer

Printed in the United States of America on acid-free paper.
10 9 8 7 6 5 4 3 2 1

Contents

NEW AND UNCOLLECTED POEMS

Second Law (1993)

His daughter went through the River singing,
but none could understand what she said.
—John Bunyan, *The Pilgrim's Progress*

... on our continents, there is no spot on
which a river may not formerly have run.
—James Hutton, *Theory of the Earth*

let this house be Endeavor and build it

No meaning was before there was a night

No mention before there was Divide

the name of the stream

a narrow stream

They retain the figure

yet the eye becomes accustomed

first the mark and then the maker

(the balance / the bow)

what little was left

Beneath

what little became

solid and so

light that path

heavy bodies travel

does the Task love the master
does the Goat love the bridge

O. adrift

in skirts and in brambles

fell asleep in this body

where depth indicates time

No one buys her ticket here. A lock of hair.

Dark and a lock of hair.

Tired to be anything but bright.

Ferryman casts over a swimming earth.

There were no oars.

There was no little dog.

striving between light

        and the force of a body

    that is light

       (every so often

lose then

       —to have known it

nailed to the space of a single I

      universing

If

as building from a limit

                              (suffers

even after metamorphosis

There is a point at the center of a bird

Envoi

        In extremes
of affection
        only to be seen

when the mind's a heart

        Seeing
by the dark grass

(your swallow)

(my bud)

        Being sure
to walk through it

To be imperfect

A crime and a gospel / is

because of you

at length
and in these

little falls

The Human Abstract (1995)

A Maiden

When I found your face on a pillow of leaves
you had already erased it. A nest so heavy
can stay in the heavens only by reversal.

By this law the knees are laced with abandon.

I said to the young man.

If watching is the manufacturer, and I lose you
what angel takes the place of a dowry
or distance in this leaf action?

Subject to like passions as we are

my soul herself, myself

a possession I could not

mistake for the man

(his language and Latin)

yet we are "taken to"

a love passage

I had hardly noticed

in the late talk of money

The work of love and the work of art

has no sleeping part

Is a drop of light

in a small silver socket,

a rosy dime

in a daylight tryst

Is *a keeper and no spender*

As seeing who is invisible:

a kind of flaxen thing

caught in stone

I obeyed and read further

"I am hemmed"

Though my heart were a pear tree
threaded with fire
Lion you leapt through me
like fineness in the boundary gene

Conductor you knit me

as isthmus   Can I touch it

Night is going 200 miles an hr

as usual   In this way we find

we are suddenly altered

If I were a day would you

like me better   Where were you

you who in a bath changed me

How to be walking

is a glorious porthole

Must I insist on an absence

more foolish and secret

When your timber's a forest

I can't see for the tree in my bed

Gentle captive, it is

a larger than murder

we tender   Fond and afire

my style and my anchor

Master there's a boat for no

lesser completion than

beauty's sweetest dress

when you look on me kind

Who am I to stop this flowing

Least of all that home mile

Sinking in the real

I dreamed there was a further island

Perhaps (how I thought you)

to salt that harness with pleasure

Lovely hero where the lovely hero bounds
an acre hidden between *eros* and its errors
Finding a dozen darts beneath the skin of
Watching the wire of a skinny flame
No other lovely hero found the back
behind her secret form of symmetry
Her gleaming difference
Her schoolish way in pretty understandings
Said   Not done   Not said   Undone
Wealthy sadness has a way of winning everyone
This is the end of my body as you know it
its superfluous penchant for love
its poorer costume, its shiny disaster

What is a maiden,

        boatswain,

but a fiery lair

and a teary citadel

By the smallest shipwreck

a daughter is laughter

Yet equalled

        as in a fable

this Gibraltar goes headlong

in a just king's love

See how his hands

are her mercy

and measure

her number and rescue

O Perseus

  Pythagoras

  Pierre

my Pierre

What rules a body's buried factions
when laundered by morning

When called by our names
although we are invisible

Sleeping I forget my animal
When the animal comes
I'm forgotten because of it

How was it called
in its own country

crossing a street
in order to come inside

from *Songs for A.*

so slender *to mean*

in dives and in arches

that I that began

to leave to resemble

So stealthy a wedding

my heart was the selfsame

This optic body

torn up   simultaneous

when I say you

is that you

the woman or the crime

I forget

& when I say you

is that you

I was about to be a syllable

I was about to fall glorious

The Human Abstract

I

Innocence shags experience and I'll never grow.
Experience catches the dove, and I'm lost.

I find you at this intimate pasture.
A number in a tree.
A gray field of otherwise.

Inventing a globe and a wheel
to turn it on.
Inventing a dress and the bird
it remembers.

This *you* of my equal and never is a restoration.

Beside the elements when they broke into picture
this is my reference to the amity of sand.

Though I skate through a vale of birds in the morning
thugs beat a carpeted path in my mind.

Who knows the moment when a vessel closes.
Whoever called light discreet.

I was beside his carriage when it meant "a glass coach."
An elaborate temper turning to accept damage.

Stems wax heavy when the face is divided

Socks of the oppressor   *When I find a wheel*

A stone occurs in less than half the time

When measured against rooftops

Archers make a body inside one yet whole

Though you have the combination

I can no longer see you through the orchard

I cast my locks on water and row with my arms

Beside this I my silence is a sister
of uncanny omissions

as though the mind were a room
a rabbit could exist behind.

A swoon where the water pours
sidelong becomes a lesson

a lantern trespassing snow
a wall torn from shadow.

"Their modeled form became an enclosure of light."

The wrestle of naming
in all our passage.

Men of the outer world dash me to bits.

This heaven is beneath earth.

If I err, I am and my error moves me

saying Child pass by here, saying "equal to me."

It was the same I unhinging
the same I throughout.

I come to this clearing but never quite omit enough.

(Three times three times)
I've forgotten my math in your footsteps.

As when the heart has lied
yet has a figure in it.

I found this in a book.
I read this by the light at the back of your head.

That's when I knew you by a starry impress
and I knew your forehead.

I knew the ground with my first feet upon it.

II (*the life of the spider*)

When *if* is *so*

that's a kind of valentine nowhere

I consider the flesh in proximity
like an anonymous "Venice"

When we finally ditched the crickets
it was clear

they were probably numbered
which is fine

but makes us murderers

We share electrons, not vistas, anyway

a boulevard, an empty purse

an outline of significance
about the knees

a diving light
a June impeachment

I know I hold a narrow to be next to

"on fire" wanders
all my body's city

Equals less than any arrow

The reader was a commoner
The assassin has the knowledge I suspected

"you" is a man
"you" writes my book

What I have is an accident
I spun my web

True, we have the bicycle

So slow is earthly progress

As "nerve" opposes confidence

Property is a form of hearing

The spider listens with her leg

Desire is a form of fastening

They were right to steal everything

We hadn't seen it

As dear as a dragonfly

Safe in captivity

The brightness of law

A wreck of its own making

Good light can be found at any altitude

Direction a by-product of wandering

Face to face, as a rule, even at nightfall

That is the function of real legs

I place the lantern inside

Human understanding is a savage construction

of dilation and resistance

This picture was taken from a false angle

The victor a transfer point

We live in a sunspot

"little o"

This picture wants keeping

Or, my treasure has fallen

from its sled

from its leg

from its web

III

In this type of you

I see I am a sequel

An illegible nightly difference

imagined, then drawn to scale

On the far road, rowing

my counterfeit

by a trick of clothing

that sequin we could never come as

if sorrow lie against this medicine

"the autumn I have is the autumn I lost"

Existing means dressing up

I do but a way to find you

an inescapable temperature

a sensitive tabloid

at the end of the angel

This love is a deer crying in a gentleman

How small is the thought
of the apparent picture

a cabinet with wrong and wonder

(the sweet string)   *I had known it*

in a different book   in a smaller triumph

Emotions are my daily actions.

Each seed has a gender.

The love of fertile ground can be a kind of phobia.

The mustard thrown to stony soil was saved.

All is fair.

IV (*a few stones for Lorine Niedecker*)

This I is an idyll
I captured the first day

the office between
the leaf and the external

Landlord I said again

you can't move a river really

yet with no apparent music
my face would pass

what bird would light
in a moving tree?

the tree I carry

what is the use
if her beauty goes

wasted on me

I said to my head
I live unburied

I am standing up

In your city
I do as your people

This nonsense has left me
unruled by examples

you Echo
you blade of grass

The egg is not by nature
better than the full crow

I am every kind of stone
but one

What I know was divided

by the weather of others

There's a kind of electricity

a fire in the first snow

A mine from the perspective of an owner

a mine as labor

I left my baby in Forest A.

(deeper, more mountainous)

the continent submerges at a distance

Death wrote a poem and I lost it

smaller than anger

larger than my head

my head filled with snow

"We build this house"

and then we live in it

Against this house I always hammering

the green of a fountain
the original honor of the thing

measured by message

I had a round of distance
till a city found me

A tinny betrayal of origin
(not stealthy not stone)

The eyebright in season
and not the storm between

I'm late and come adrift

Turneresque (2003)

Autographeme

A thought on the lip
of little sand island

An easy messenger
who forgot where to go

I came to laugh
in a dirty garden

A thwarted pauselessness
considering pearls

I was fluent in salamander

Everything wrote itself onto skin
with a tangled blowing

An opal eye looking down
on an errant package

A sky wrung of tint

What is the meaning
of this minor error?

The reflecting pool
no one could read

A beach fire snagged me
with its bright emergent eye

My colony sought revolt
in every yard

The present was a relic
of a past I was older than

Taking its language, I became an abridgement
of whatever I contained

A social imperative of silky fears

I wanted air
I wanted the balloon

Darkness flaked down like bottle glass
invented by a poor oily sea

A house made of soup

Others formed an invisible order
felt in every part

The male of the species was
louder than the female

Females made the mush
a sound of offstage sweeping

Boys played a game of torment
and sleepy forgiveness

while girls read their books on the rocks
containers of a solar plot

Little bird, fox on a string

A caravan of foreign number
staging death

So?

A smudge against the smallest dress
buried creature, of sly erasures

in the storied night, long *e*
cricketing awake, asleep

Sonnet

To live in someone
else's music (the musician
not the composer is free)
a divine contention
like the damp carpet
of liquored olivia trees
(something my favorite you
would say)
finding in a hollow day
a winter keeper
a paper woman
caught in the torrent
not quite falling

Carrying an atmosphere
beaten out like sound
a still life of amnesty
on the little lane
Trees are safely tucked
below the wires
a darkness carried
out of childhood
other kindnesses
"I looked"
and fell to

Unable to hire oneself
for labor or to know
the green, braided thing
someone sees
inside you

Forgetting your grasp
or "words"
in a paper understanding
a paper flap of happy self
Your dream above your head
like comic weather

The teacher's love
of someone's children
a flash of light
in white air

So loving love
we lack science
and in ourselves
touch up the little
teacher's picture

Thinking through
a desperate wedge
of indivisible ink
we fall in filaments
an uncontrolled breeze
nutsy, bottled
forged & forgot
Crawling (not climbing) down
netted, I bet

As proud & difficult as Greek
a vigil (or Virgil)
kept bright
waiting to happen
Your father walking
toward your mother
as you briefly look away
then follow like a nonsense syllable
Ma. Pa.

Figs of lost thought
rainy differences and non-glides
feverish in girlways
The tenuous escape of a patient
nodding, obstinate
jeweled or pinked
A pilling station
(laughing, molten)
behind a gay exterior
or broad caplet
too tough to swallow

Our daphne dissipates
a young mist
Must she follow
the if/then into ether
A little myth
in the grass
never hurt anyone
or so
they said
"little apple cake"

A fateful history
beginning to clang
To hunt the doe
in a row of air
Things like sage or virtue
A reader desires
to be crushed by sun
I defile books but
I don't drink beer
Bent into a box
I wrastled fair
I & I
to make it new
or rue among the rose

Anyone has half a life
like salt in groggy sunlight
a dreamed acceleration
forgetfully & fully
there: arena's
circumstance
a textile jolt
awaiting debt
asurf in drift
on peels or wheels

Forgetting the tumbled
sheen of home
we calculate a rescue
out of summer
Lovely missions
in early green
A dream of love
dearest curtain
painted just
beyond the face
a trembling show
attending moonlight
the verso alive
against you

Grammar is coral
a gabled light
against the blue
a dark museum
Durable thing

I find you in a string
I find you every-
where I'm writing
on a leaf, a
satire of flesh-
liness   A tree
is pure intent
and mindlessness
as once, the it
was he or she

Without an arch
triumph is a fantasy
of daily warfare
lunging into nightly airs
Iron can't protect
a feeble word, I'm
less confident
than butter   The blind
limits of a ragged
suggestion: to follow
like an Astor, to belong
to dirt, like a question

The Tree of Personal Effort

after Charles Rennie Mackintosh

The lost highway of ornament fades into origin. Ship-wrecks return like magnets to their builders. In the tree of personal effort, a balloon is lodged or branches are basketed. What did we think we dared to sail away from, an unread book, an aspirin? My body knew I was anchored to earth with flesh. Build a bigger bellows if you want to rise above your life. So sighs the pilot's cloud of word. To imply or intone the whole possibility of human sun. The rose rose unknit with spring. A dragonfly in your hand for luck.

Van Tromp, Going About to Please His Masters, Ships a Sea, Getting a Good Wetting

after J. M. W. Turner

Constancy scribbles itself out in waves: a revisionary litter of brown light. Fleety with anchor and going abroad, a fulcrum pulls to left of center. A slap in the face of a sail. A device spies down a-swing in salt & gunpowder, an amber passage. Horizons cast their calm tunes. It doesn't take a traitor to overturn a boat. It wouldn't take such amber to blue up the sky. A heavy craft in wordy water, taking on a master. Van Tromp at the prow, asunder surrounded, clothes himself and sets the sail to follow out his inner course. What is his fiction to the boot of manacles, what is I to the future of pain, of boy, of boat life. Afield and legion. The opposite of grass.

The Young Blake

sleeps into heaven with his lamps on, finishing explan-
atory negotiations for a while. *Desert the enemy.* Star
formations, sandstone understanding, rock time in gen-
eral, whatever. Latching onto ecstasy, words that change
on waking, clover as a syrup of spring mind. Working
off a deficit of sleep or cash, you know who your friends
are. Singled out in traffic, lurching into light, having
lunch. You're a little one with sand in your eyes, with
green on your horn, with milk on your chin. With flow-
ering ears and hearsay.

Arthur in Egypt

Where do you go after a season in Denver, walking through Africa in shoes of sand. My name was a green flash on the glassy horizon. My pen leaked until there was nothing else to say. When my feet were gone I rowed ashore, beached on the word, *pure*. What happens once can never come again, even in a dream. So I moved on, or it passed through.

The Wolfman

A man with a cane has made a long trip. He's unstrung, coming home. Trapped, in agony, he heals in moony thickets. He gives away pentagrams. He tiptoes through fog. He's as good natured as Jesus. An errant son with an aversion to pity, he's reluctant to love. He shoots paper ducks but can't hit the canine. In a plaster forest he's riddled by replicas. He needs a shrink. He's bound to the gypsy by a terrible necklace. You can't protect everyone from yourself.

A Woman's Face

Doctors sculpt a monster to disprove everything. Scaling mountains, she forgives herself the climbs of youth. Nothing can stop her dark mouth. She governs boys carelessly, she stars all the time. Acts accrue against her inner caning. She lifts and shoots in furs, criming her way to newness, men. She carries herself like a parcel over waterfalls bejeweled in salt. Her breath is honeysuckle in winter. Mourning doves carry her by the shoulders. Shaking curls against her neck, caught in a lie, she mines inwardly for change. Her forehead glows like cream above the Austrian ego. She can read.

On Dangerous Ground

Jim's a bad one whining down a concrete river slick with night. Another wrong punch and he'll be badgeless. A bloodhound sent to hicksville on a sleeper, he stumbles on a country missile. She feels her way to the smoothest things, she builds an indelible fire. Her brother's heart is an inward tree, but he's got blood on his hands. Love gropes them more than blossoms. Jim's been wrong before, but now he's pinned by the discreteness of her body in the dark. There's no turning back for a cop with snow in his shoes. She leans into his face: the hardness of water. The fluidity of land. The total radiance of faces in a mine. He sinks against her ivy wall. There's no telling where she'll lead.

Kiss Me Deadly

Christina Rossetti papers London with canary flyers. The next thing she knows, she's falling into headlights, lying in toxic sedge. She's dead all right. She's swallowed the key into the language of America. She's invested in advertising. It's a nuclear secret, a box of smack, and she's its beachhead. She's come from the dead to be remembered, and if she has to kill someone along the way, that's poetry.

September 9

It's turneresque in twilight. The word comes at me
with its headlights on, so it's revelation and not death.
I figure I'm halfway home though I've only started.
Nothing is moving but me: I'm a blackbird. The neigh-
bor's in labor, but so am I, pushing against the road.
Physics tells us nothing is lost, but I've been copping
time from death and can't relent for every job the stars
drop on my back.

Elegy

The day I drove

in a driving rain
from realism to impressionism

a moving hillside fooled the town

What does it take
to make a happy ant?

a dropped lozenge
on the damp step

bumping into a friend
in the daily grind

avoiding death

Still you slip away
in a desert hospital

and cannot see to see

Hawthorne's hand
against your hair

the stumbling blue
of windowed air

What unknown slippered thing of x is thou
a dirty engine shooting out the star
a decoy aurora'd in fig
I myself
in plain flesh, answer

The soul's a fine thing
less than feathers
free to glitter
in no-light night

a petticoat of sand
the mind's a hinge
a roughly chestnut arsenal
a little box of nothing
an incidental rose

If a dove spoke
lifted into goldleaf

—leaving for home
like a fox through mint

a canned geranium
like what you see is—

would we understand

I hobble into sun-gray air
to feel the carbon in my hair

Fins of centuries brushing by

I felt the grass's poem
blown against me
like a fake harp

like the harmony of deluge
before I seen you
subtly from behind
the dewy lumber of my eye

An Ozymandias
permanent as plastic
forever underneath

A green sky figured
flickered out against
a life given up to cement

Where's the organ an animal forgives with
Where's my "heart" within the cells I cotton to

To flurry and ark the lumber of sky
a boat of white enamel, a step into the yard

like a tin adventure
blown forward in a crowd

Threading a life
of levered paradox

snowy patterns of the arch composer

in feathered mud
to lean aground

to leave behind
an almost empty ivy mind

feet that are roots
a piece of string
that is a mountain

a flight of color
disturbed into line

When I was a fish
I didn't have to answer

being in a bush or hand
a face in locomotion

that crashes in between

Book of Matthew

for Matthew Shepard (1976–1998)

Here's a text that's mixed with others
wired into snocone snow
what you see and what you get
a block from the Union Pacific
against a ten-mile fence of news

My great-uncle was a train man
strictly steam, he never got over
the Twentieth Century

My brother was born in Casper
the wind was a joke
a mean metal syllogism
with nowhere to go

You've been indexed
& written in pencil on bedroom walls
& like Shelley, writ in light
in a mind the size of a coin
conceived as memory
the beginning of sorrows

from *Drive*

What last broke against leaf, under leaf-bearing mind?
So little disturbs the sea by comparison. Do you mind?
Finding a reflected mountain is really a shadow, a tree
is beneath its color, the shore a mirage. A real boat in
imaginary water. Yellow fall, green gilled. Trees have
the only real land-legs. Consider our end. The lights are
dry in daylight, up in the dipper, the Hammer, scor-
pion, the Hurricane. The kid's fire is hidden, under-
neath. To crawl out from under. It's dirt. Don't win.
Don't put it out.

What you rise out of may not be dirt, but what you breathe must be air. On an indigo chart, we drive without a future, left to wish outside the forward rush of things. Who would not leave the mess for the illumination, the culture for the poem? Believe in inconstancy, a colorist. Forgetting the orangist is only a pomologist, not a painter sent home for lack of design. The night's a plateau. Where would we be in desert night, deserted. Constantinopilized. Oranged.

The day left off with a kind of singing "bang." Goldenrod in a small sea-like air, specific and unbroken. I cannot favor hunger or its alternatives. I cannot describe salt. In a parallel universe does anything intersect the confused blossoming blueness of a wall that is not sea, not goldenrod, but the paper fastening of you, standing against it? I favor concrete between our rage and its mirage. Its broken line. Catch the flying saucer but spit out its metal mystery. Adore the big green nothing of the past, the rationing of calm late in the century, like the arches of a brick heart, letting go.

Meteoric Flowers (2006)

A poem is a meteor.
　　　　　　—Wallace Stevens

look, soldiers of Ulysses,
your spears
have begun to flower too!
　　　　　　—Charles Reznikoff

The Similitude of This Great Flower

These vines are trim, I take them down. I have my mother's features in my heart, the darkest gem, tripping in the tar, an affinity for Iceland. The world is clanking: noun, noun, noun. Sand in the shoe doesn't make you an oyster. This river runs constantly. "The similitude of this great flower," its violent fame. Forfeit your interests while moonlight chucks the sun. Is the dog behind glass, glassed in? Heaven's voice has hell behind it. I'm looking at the evil flower, a fly in the keyhole trying to read the wall. It says we haven't died despite the cold, it sells the green room's sweat and laughter. It's misty in the dream. It says you promised to go on.

Sympathetic Inks

In the middle of the brook you surprised me: summer
fox, metacomet, gingerboy. The point of the story was,
does the fox eat the goose, does the gingerboy melt, can
she fly to shore? I'm crawling toward the corn, kicking
open the field. I see the face in flower and want to draw
it, I chop the tree without thinking, a book or a subtle
lean-to. What if we were standing by the boat, like
Seabiscuit deciding whether to run the lane or drift into
forbidden meadows? So gods fall to earth with tender
irritation. What we love in time kills us, poppy dear,
sugaring our skulls with backward music.

Her Mossy Couch

I stain lengthwise all I touch. The world is so touching, seen this way, in fleshtones, aggrieved, gleaming as the lights go out, looking in to the crease of relativity. We've seen this before, why? Triumph arches over us like bad emotion. We were supposed to feel more connected to it, we were supposed to feel humanly moved by imaginary strings. All the words in the world are moving pictures to the dizzy ear, fleas, inadequate deceptions of nocturnal hair, pushing buttons, pushing papers, pushing pedals up the long hill. Who could get over the blatant radiance of a name like Doris Day, throwing your finest features into political relief, a warehouse in the shadow of apples and streams?

A Description of the Poison Tree

The girl is a grid, silked with phenomena, an early promise broken into clover. An owl bends both its eyes to this object. Her desire for shining, a symptom of this bashfulness. Among the lower orders a W is sibilant. A physical lantern, honey in the ear. A larger bird's cry may be hidden from view by a broad enough table. I find her in delirium about to pass for mad. The letter S between the teeth, pushed back into the mouth, as when confronted she has pointed to the word "paper." She doesn't want to be the dollar sign, split and smirking, living in a desert of bolted-down things.

Grateful as Asparagus

The house of mirth is casting its shadows. My bureau, my agency, a wall of sliding glass. Without its leaky reverie, the face is a shield. Who wouldn't love the sycamore in spite of its skin? For a minute the fountain was an indoor labyrinth, a garden gone wild into perfect order. See the bleeding ankle? The meat of the body left alone to run the house. In the company of A or B, in the company of M or W, unfixed by science, a leaning spectacle. The delicate column, the poppied hill.

The Oldest Part of the Earth

Girl is notational, she's an index. From the couch I see Mary saying yes and no, he and she. We're only clay: blossom machines. Sure I'll carry your latest worry, sorry it's not dripping in your favorite green. Our cheeks are marked with leafy stains. What lasts forever won't survive its station any more than that junebug can translate through the screen. We're living on, anyway, immaculate lawns. Neo-forsythia.

Verses Omitted

Belimbed as a willow
I'm burning with wingedness

Our midnight special
launched toward precipity

Don't let another season
make a joke of piracy

I swim to shore
every day

unfashionably mirrored
with iridescent moss

Even in terror
surely we survive

the scheduled collapse
of yesterday's cakes

On the Resemblance of Some Flowers to Insects

A smoky vessel drifts east like a slippery elixir. By simple rotation night collapses with its head in the dirt, though from the heights it appears more like cubist swagger. Suddenly curtains. What lives in a room takes on the spirit of the room. This is true even of television. Imagine deciding the gulley a life will follow as if choosing breakfast over diligent labor. I don't remember my first brush with pollen, yet I've watched words flower sideways across your mouth. In a month we'll be dizzily older. Moths will leave singed paper on the stoop. Is this my design? An ant crosses my shadow so many times looking for its crumb, I think it's me who's needlessly swaying. Its path is busy eloquence while I'm merely armed, like a chair leaving the scent of large things on the breeze.

The Principal Catastrophe

I thought I was reading but suddenly I'm read. Some kind of artist then, painting his targets. Distinct or indistinct sensation? I prefer clarity when I can afford it. So what if another flower plagiarized the rosary? I'd pick up a dime in private or a quarter in public, money's always been "dirty," some kind of death wish. Sure I'd like to own a pet, not own but take care of, not a monkey or donkey, but something that loves you like money or luck. Not a puppy made of flowers but like music, in dog years.

Of Which I Shall Have Occasion to Speak Again

Look at the base, asking to be stolen. Someone in the cash family, staining our hands. Who thought in this idyll we'd be lying on needles? Like what's-her-name in the movie about the doctor, so unlike a shepherd. A loosely valid enterprise, god and his pair of dice. This meadow, I swear, cashes in on leaflessness. We're sliding in the outfield, sure it's alive. I'm drawn to the warmth of what doesn't belong to me, waking up on the bus with money in my pants.

Pictures Connected by a Slight Festoon of Ribbons

When the ship is in danger, a bell can be the most familiar sound. Traveling by coach or the disastrous locomotive refinements of wind. Of important motionless conversation, the mouth's wicked noise, an internal sensation of ten and of apparent fever, an alcove of Lear. To voluntarily dissolve before a lesser lens, to bark and blither till the end in drunkenness, or as a cottage trembles above the snow with a surprise like joy.

Viewless Floods of Heat

So much for swans. Or, having lost it, "add this city to my weather." Being vernal, I've had it with desire. A winter scene middled and rung, with its brilliant use of stupefaction. Something closer, a less gratuitous tower. Incumbent lilies seem to own their consequence, someone's on her back. What do you think of our soldiers, Elizabeth, trying not to be disappointed? I'm not even parked at the gold-rimmed lake, forget about the china. The body is always softer than its image. Shined up, collectible, all it imagined.

The Ghost of Hamlet

Remembering the weather doesn't mean we make it happen. A king shows up like boredom, almost chic it's so real. Our species puts us down beyond the trees, a colophon for everything that's broken in the grass. Folks pan out like zeroism on the grid, the state is red or blue. Flags are in stitches, factoring out the latest breeze, the "she" of elation. Of further benefit, America owns the moon. Even something simple can be squared to death. Try to scale this pyramid while it's cooking into glass. Prepare yourselves for a rigorous chill, be urgently chiffoned.

Departure of the Nymphs Like Northern Nations Skating on the Ice

At borders everywhere, this is what we fly with, this poppy I'm pouring, coming down like tar. To wonder if the list is earned, to be looking for an island, just one flowering minute. Some powder I was reaching for floats above my hand. Why not crab the fence when you can find it, why not pose before the fire? I catch the flood with my toe. Flowery carpets floor the idyll. Even if I don't write it down, I'm just a form of tuning. I take this green to build my shirt. I do this work to word you.

Verses Omitted by Mistake

Were I invited
to draft that flower

an unfixed wilder thing
would fix upon my palm

Those wolves are numbered
to a government rifle

If Lucy rules
the castle of indolence

I joy to dream
a more fortunate planet

Bright o'er the Floor

Suddenly the daisycutter someone was waiting for. I hear the keys like modern ice on its way to hell. We safecrackers have come here for the job, a gasp among luggage. Useless wings. Hook & eye. Assemblage as forgiveness. Get in the car on collaborative ankles. We're rowing like Greeks before those trees turn to treason, erased of all their writing.

Solar Volcanos

If I appear to play the violin, it's only to keep my head on. Everything heavy falls in September, a fire truck lost on polar seas. I see the blueness in our thinking, lit up from behind. Turning to salt, turning to stone, I'm turning into water. When my blood plays cold, just think where my face has been. If I can speak for the entire space station I'd say we've suffered less than most. Maybe this moment is a test of coloration, an ashy mountainside made to look like dawn.

Loud Cracks from Ice Mountains Explained

The alarm in my heart is made of silly brass, some of us can't help but mourn the end of Lorca. Rain continues into rain, fire interrupts my car with all the better reason of the forest. I see misfortune in the eye of real weather. Pronouns understand their game before we join the histories that betray us. The happening of summer, all verb upon the land. Could word belie its little clouds, Montblanc would storm against the poet's skin. His mansion is her excess love, a careful avalanche of we and they. A footstep bound for weary day awaits its sound upon the grain.

Ancient Subterranean Fires

When I crossed the road, I burned with the heat of its traffic. Time as movement, a government of rushes. All those itching satellites, blind among the dreaming guns. A bee in its lace is the author of something. Easy work is out there, just beyond the mines. A cab into heroic legend, the first of its kind. To look back on gasoline as hoof and leaf. A moving eye, scrolling through the weeds. Just another carnivore frozen at the spring. As dirty as heaven, a skeleton key.

Plundering Honey

Fluent in applejack, I'm knocked off my horse but gaining on liberty. No one spends all his life tanked, what do I mean "spends"? What do I mean "his"? I'm wiping my face on your sleeve as if I'm looking through my own sun. We live in the flower, so I can't taste anything. It's that hot, Tex, a new kind of glue. O, I think therefore I green the grass I'm pinned upon.

Accidental Breezes

What sudden rhetoric trembles at the door? I see clouds reflected in the gutter, but they're still clouds. Having never shot a deer, I ride the hill like homeward ire. Out-paced, unpetaled, a boomerang of star fury: all my busted rigor. Whatever it is arranges itself for capture, the wormwood box, ghost of a chance. No one's alone anymore. A name slides home, two words dashed to silly alchemy, a sun uncorked of glory. What little monster have I made, to favor love of all that's said?

Primeval Islands

This I, this me, I'm speaking from a book. That brain that taught me delicious things, forgivable trains, a signal business. I don't want to be tragic, even to the gold-leafed bug. I, Walt Whitman, with Texas in my mouth. Dismiss this fantasy in favor of our startled shade. I remembered my tricks and what they did. Even apples aren't free. Our life against the midnight lens: poor Crusoe on Mars. I'm walking through this wall of air to comfort my senate.

Ferns, Mosses, Flags

We all live under the rule of Pepsi, by the sanctified waters of an in-ground pond. Moss if it gathers is a sign of shifting weathers, the springing scent of consensual facts. A needle's knowing drops into focus while you sleep in its haystack. A boy on the road, a guileless girl disguised as a brook. Even trees deploy their shadows, embossing your skin with the sound of freedom breaking. No one mistakes choice for necessity. Look at the pilgrims in your filmy basket, illustrious eyebrows colored with chalk. The lake is panicking. A latent mystery detected in sepia is quaking to its end. I too have a family astonished, unsaintly. Asleep, I saw them. A porcelain dome insisting on trust, jeweled with telepathy. I don't know how to pour this country from a thinner vessel. Or account for the era of martian diplomacy. Little bridges connect every century, seasonally covered with the rime of empire. Can you successfully ignore the eyes in the painting? Can you recount the last three images in reverse order? I read the picture and did what it told me, ducking through the brush with my tablet and pen, following some star.

All the Paintings of Giorgione (2006)

The birth of Paris

Susanna and Daniel, in the hands of an undisclosed corporation

The savior as a boy, playing with a ball, attributed to Andrea del Sarto, thought by Oscar Wilde to be Paris with the golden apple

Homage to a Poet, sold under the title Solomon and his Servants

Gypsy and Soldier, formerly known as Mercury and Isis

The Madonna, reading

Under the soldier's figure x-rays reveal an earlier outline of a bathing woman

The mosaic of the ground against the mosaic of her arm

The Three Philosophers, later identified as Three Wise Men, in the possession of the Archduke Leopold Wilhelm

Portrait of a Lady, formerly the property of Prince Lichnowsky at Kuchelna and later Lord Melchett at Romsey

Stories of Adonis: "his birth, ...his sweet embraces with Venus...his killing by a boar...." (lost)

The Holy Family at the National Gallery

The Allendale Nativity, once called a derivation

Portrait of Laura in the inventory of 1659

Night in the home of Taddeo Contarini

Night in the home of Vincenzo Beccaro

Susanna and Daniel could be The Adulteress described as "for sale" in 1612

The Ambush (lost)

The Dresden Horoscope, thought to be a copy

The Head of an Old Man, once attributed to Perugino

Portrait of an ancient King (lost)

Portrait of Doge Agostino Barbarigo (lost)

Judith in the collection of Catherine the Great, formerly ascribed to Raphael

Shepherd with pipe, acquired by Charles I, believed to be a copy

Nude woman and shepherd with pipe (lost)

The doctoring of cats (lost)

Twelve pictures portraying the story of Psyche (lost)

Large head of Poliphemus wearing a hat (lost)

Episode of the Emperor Friedrich kissing the foot of Pope Alexander III (lost)

The Judgment of Solomon and The Trial of Moses, once attributed to Bellini

Half-length of a nude "in green cloth" (lost)

Young man in fur coat (lost)

Portrait of a German of the Fulchera family "seen from the side and turning about"

Madonna with Saint Jerome and other figures (lost)

Madonna with Saints Anthony of Padua and Roch, believed by Velázquez to be the work of Pordenone

Madonna with Saints Francis and Liberale, badly restored

Portrait of a captain in armor (lost)

Three-quarter length figure of Saint Sebastian (lost)

Half-figure of Saint Jerome reading a book (lost)

At this point in our story, relief disappears

Allegories of human life and half-figures: "nurse with child, armed warrior," a "young man disputing with philosophers, among merchants and an old woman," "an antique nude" (lost)

Grotesques in chiaroscuro and children overlooking the Canal at Santa Maria Zobenigo (lost)

Three portraits upon the same canvas

Portrait of Caterina Cornaro, seen in the house of Giorgio Vasari (lost)

Portrait of Leonardo Loredano when he was Doge (lost)

The great Consalvo himself, armed

Portrait of a youth in armor, in which his hand is reflected (lost)

Bust of a woman in gypsy clothing with her right hand on a book (lost)

Antonia da Bergamo who, having gripped a dagger, is about to kill herself to protect her virginity (lost)

Portrait of Giovanni Bernardi's father-in-law (lost)

A nude sleeping Venus, with Cupid at her feet and a small bird in her hand, finished by Titian

The portrait of Giovanni as a young man and in the same picture the portrait of the master who was his teacher...(lost)

David's head, said to be his own portrait, with hair coming down to the shoulders

The larger head of a man, "holding in his hand the red beret of a Commander" (lost)

The head of a cherub or boy with hair like goatskin (lost)

Half-length figure of a soldier, armed but not wearing his helmet (lost)

Shadows on a hillside refuse the universal as the landscape moves away

The dead Christ upon his tomb, supported by an angel, mistakenly identified with the Dead Christ of Treviso

The nude St Jerome sitting in the desert in the moonlight, copied from a canvas by Zorzo of Castelfranco (lost)

A nude woman copied from Zorzo, reclining and turned (lost)

Two small paintings on goatskin, in vermilion, by Giulio Campagnola

Some do not ascribe The Sleeping Venus to Giorgione at all

A country landscape may be merely Giorgionesque

The head of a young shepherd with fruit in his hand
(lost)

Head of a youth holding an arrow, generally identified
as the "three-quarter length figure of Saint Sebastian"
(lost)

From behind a wall a hundred yards away, the wind
brings us the scent of oleander

The Venetian moves away from math

Rigorous perspective collapses into tone

Self-portrait as David holding Goliath's head, between
a knight and a soldier (lost)

Half-length figure of Mr. Hieronimo, reading (lost)

The portrait of the very same Hieronimo in arms,
showing his back down to the waist, and turning his
head (lost)

Aeneas and Anchises in Hell, repainted and altered

Breath moves the foliage

This is the moment when painting becomes painting

From now on the world will be expressed as "visible
distance"

So matter is indented toward its perfect prose

The figure of a woman with flowers in her hand, with "the figure of Vulcan whipping Eros" (lost)

Portrait of an Old Woman, thought to be the artist's mother

And so one may speak of "my Giorgione" and not another's

One cannot do more than refer to its intimate attributes, to one's concept of style

Its pictorial language, his Leonardismo

The expensive music behind the Storm at Sea

Look for the line separating breadth from opulence

An allegory of Chastity, now believed to be a copy

The Virgin of the Rocks

Theory of a revolution

FROM

Address (2011)

Address

I is to they
as river is to barge
as convert to picket line
sinker to steamer
The sun belongs to I
once, for an instant
The window belongs to you
leaning on the afternoon
They are to you
as the suffocating dis-
appointment of the mall
is to the magic rustle
of the word "come"
Turn left toward the mountain
Go straight until you see
the boat in the driveway
A little warmer, a little stickier
a little more like spring

Nocturne

I'm thinking of
the heat in the reins
a gear in love with itself
two parts that fit
I'm thinking about your face:
there's nothing to invent
Driven to distraction
or just walking there
The edge of my mind
against the edge of yours
An astrolabe isn't thinking
of a concrete lane
or unconquerable interior
Abiding by its class
and country church, a kitsch picture
is not "sincerity"
though I am native to it
A nation has this sound
of being born   The human
is not its ill-begotten ad
A hemisphere is not your hair
in its Parisian rooms
An astrolabe is not
a metaphor for love
though love contain the mortal roots
of congress, like a peasant
inside the name you give its ruins

Friday

Coming to you
from a jumbled dream

My heart caves in
the better to see you with

I'm thinking on the bright side
while looking for my keys

I've never seen a body
floating to the ceiling

in the big room
of the post office

A word is a symptom
of what can't be described

A promise, a premise
held open like a door

So I didn't find mercy
or it didn't find me

It's always personal
like the failure of a knee

A brassy rebuttal
clowning in the street

Your footprint on the planet
pinned down by outer space

A Species Is an Idea (1)

Leaving my umbrella
I left everything behind

That dog, an emblem
of my dirty self

All this reflection
amounting to shadows

Ink eats the page:
it's Chemistry against the Forest

What train are you on
with all these thoughts?

What bitter landscape
the better to hear you with?

Its stepless grid
is suddenly a corridor

You write this down
You're at the end of it

Flow Chart

You take the sun personally
like a coin in a purse
Anything can change
in a blink, an eye
becomes a storm
The hole closes over
the river, the air
in the cut you leave behind
The love you broke into
then couldn't patch up
Words sail over
your finest antennae
Even the warmth of a poem
suggests a proximate danger
Wild mushrooms
Camouflage

The Witch

A witch can charm milk from an ax handle.

A witch bewitches a man's shoe.

A witch sleeps naked.

"Witch ointment" on the back will allow you to fly through the air.

A witch carries the four of clubs in her sleeve.

A witch may be sickened at the scent of roasting meat.

A witch will neither sink nor swim.

When crushed, a witch's bones will make a fine glue.

A witch will pretend not to be looking at her own image in a window.

A witch will gaze wistfully at the glitter of a clear night.

A witch may take the form of a cat in order to sneak into a good man's chamber.

A witch's breasts will be pointed rather than round, as discovered in the trials of the 1950s.

A powerful witch may cause a storm at sea.

With a glance, she will make rancid the fresh butter of her righteous neighbor.

Even our fastest dogs cannot catch a witch-hare.

A witch has been known to cry out while her husband places inside her the image of a child.

A witch may be burned for tying knots in a marriage bed.

A witch may produce no child for years at a time.

A witch may speak a foreign language to no one in particular.

She may appear to frown when she believes she is smiling.

If her husband dies unexpectedly, she may refuse to marry his brother.

A witch has been known to weep at the sight of her own child.

She may appear to be acting in a silent film whose placards are missing.

In Hollywood the sky is made of tin.

A witch makes her world of air, then fire, then the planets. Of cardboard, then ink, then a compass.

A witch desires to walk rather than be carried or pushed in a cart.

When walking a witch will turn suddenly and pretend to look at something very small.

The happiness of an entire house may be ruined by witch hair touching a metal cross.

The devil does not speak to a witch. He only moves his tongue.

An executioner may find the body of a witch insensitive to an iron spike.

An unrepentant witch may be converted with a little lead in the eye.

Enchanting witchpowder may be hidden in a girl's hair.

When a witch is hungry, she can make a soup by stirring water with her hand.

I have heard of a poor woman changing herself into a pigeon.

At times a witch will seem to struggle against an unknown force stronger than herself.

She will know things she has not seen with her eyes. She will have opinions about distant cities.

A witch may cry out sharply at the sight of a known criminal dying of thirst.

She finds it difficult to overcome the sadness of the last war.

A nightmare is witchwork.

The witch elm is sometimes referred to as "all heart." As in, "she was thrown into a common chest of witch elm."

When a witch desires something that is not hers, she will slip it into her glove.

An overwhelming power compels her to take something from a rich man's shelf.

I have personally known a nervous young woman who often walked in her sleep.

Isn't there something witchlike about a sleepwalker who wanders through the house with matches?

The skin of a real witch makes a delicate binding for a book of common prayer.

When all the witches in your town have been set on fire, their smoke will fill your mouth. It will teach you new words. It will tell you what you've done.

Vernacular Architecture

Seeing to the creature:
leaning, bending down
What grass is tendered
in what state of the union?
Any body can be unionized
A governed love for the people
isn't special
The government of love
is to believe itself unwritten
Love's office is devotion
to the ungoverned, like justice
somewhere else, in a while
A school beside its architect
A child next to a picture
The family in its tunnels
Pure products feel their power
to feed the engine
Their movement a document
that totters into being
written with their elbows
and their hands
Here is what I found today
or what I am

Ruskin

I hear the whistle blowing
but I cannot see the train
The wrong buildings
are coming down to meet me
An oily noise waving its petition
in the face of what a future
So my book becomes a road
drifting casually toward a lake
The road talks to the stonebreaker
in a private language
inaudible by carriage
A hand transposes
the work of the eye
until it cannot tell
which side is up
Dear Rose, I think
that I would like to be
a weapon like a pillow
in the hands of an angry girl
A building in the shape of a cloud
that takes the shape of a galleon
shaped like a bow
of hickory or witchhazel
or the willow that weeps against
this pillow-thought of you

A Species Is an Idea (2)

The vine is just a vine
a substitute for nothing:
little mitten
bellwether friend

Or you, my landscape
a sensory derangement
next to Ireland's forgeries
the dream of her gigantic ear

on the poem's longest coastline
The poem that is America
America a prophecy
like reason in atomic winter

We think its magic wheel
is but a dress
that calls this city home
Unpeopled, architectural

January

My office alerts me
I have only so much time

Prosperity is just around
that hairpin turn

In this way the poem
lays its hand against your head

Its words are using you
to power-down the view

Thinking like a cloth
means taking on a darker black

I'm that thirsty
in the middle of the day

This bent hour finds
its way into your hand

Like a cane or a whip
like a feather or a pen

It only exists
in one place at a time

Extended Forecast

If lace in the machine
then air in the head of a lilac

The face up close
is up against the minted wind

Overseen like labor
overlooked like a valley

Triptik

I'm browsing through
this crop circle

with Rousseau
in the woods

A confounded geography
of accidental history

Little leaf in the scrub
scrubbed away by the current

Green against the glass
and grass against the silver

A hair falls to the boat launch
like good money after bad

You look for the beginning
of the poem

between the moving x's
of the bridge

Wherefore my masterwork
of plated opulence

The constant flowering
of our downward mobility

This is the I
I've learned to speak to

way, way out there
in the luggage and cabbage

A tripwire on the field
of Great Ideas:

stone from a mountain
box without glue

ingenious bobbin
into dawn

The machine day assists you
with its simple fittings

To drive so as not
to touch the world

To oversee and not to hear
its irregular sob

Choosing to be looking
so as not to be buying

This errand won't deliver you
as you break apart the flower

To rise to this
to speak its fury

Classified

Will trade fountain pen for outboard motor
a trembling nightfall for government bonds
Will trade this grievance for a moment of silence
that wooded tavern for my aimless youth
Will trade potable water for loyal army
Fabergé egg for interpretation of dreams
Will trade heirloom lilacs for three cords of wood
Will trade this meadow for a person-sized piece of shade
Will trade fluttering leaf for a career in baseball
Will trade class warfare for a place to lay my head
Will trade a life of crime for a month in the country
a decorative pear for a clean, dry pillow
a wheelbarrow for an end to all that

In Strength Sweetness

in the wind / an inky air

in the air / finchness

in the ink / a stone

in the winter / winter

in the nest / in the piney

in the tree / filigree

in the great / bye and bye

in the worm / William Blake

in the fall / fortune

in the ocean / a figure

in canvas / the grain

in the apartment / a body

in the mountain / its making

in the cottage / a fable

in the mind / its miniature

in the seed / a sun

in the fist / a question

in the question / an expedition

in the expedition / a bank

in the dollar / a seal

in the seal / another seal

in the sand / a massacre

in the blood / spirit

in the word / your mouth

in the tale / its labyrinth

in the lion / the bee

in the bee / a plain

in the plan / a city

in your city / its anger

in your anger / a harbor

in your harbor / a boat

in the boat / open sea

New and Uncollected Poems

The Completist

Concrete is not
completeness
A dream will
shake its mind
as light may be
unfinished with
its day

The poem was not
about the wind or
waking, a beginning
or an end

The peonies are
finished, so am I
but not the dream
its closure welling
up out of the dark

To walk some
new world's un-
precedented residue
or find its arc
to build a shelter

I didn't think my art
could take it, its light
against my chest
would be an end
of architecture

The tree has made
a wall of green
as in your dream
the peonies have
blown, the lilacs
have forgiven not
the blast of columbine
Forget-me-nots
overrun by lilies

Even in the cool
of day, it is not
cool, still a thought
of what's to come

Even dead things
have their pattern
Even the best part
ripples out
and disappears

Survey

No one uses the running path anymore
There's nowhere to run to
The station next to the tracks
is labeled SPRING
Why fence off a river?
I used to worry I'd never get
warm again
They worry their cul-de-sac
will hide a human cloud
with a cart full of cans
I worry the beaver pattern
won't retake the shore
How far out could I walk
through the marsh?

I worry the neck was broken
but the body lived
I worry Union Street
is a dead end
I worry moss grows
on both sides of the tree
that we are headed into slavery

I worry the island
is getting farther away
that the song won't stop
so we'll never really hear it
I worry the grass
won't green again
that the sidewalk
will attack my teeth

I don't worry that words will fail me
but that I will fail words
Even the word *tree* has a contract,
the word *word*, the word *you*
Will *we* ever have a contract?
I worry the propane depot
will explode as we pass
and I worry about the dog next door

I worry the wheat won't tassel
that the weak things will become weaker
that witches'-broom
will take over Wisconsin
I worry that my youth was wasted
in obedience, which it was

I worry there is not enough modern
pollen for the ancient bees
I worry the shoelace
its oncoming train
I worry about gunpowder
and tiny bits of nails
and the liquid softness of the eye
I worry that the bus will leave
five minutes early
that there will be no place dry to sleep

I dream an archive, not a courthouse
I worry that winter will expose the nest
that the air conditioner
will poison the eggs
I worry that I will faint
where no one can hear me fall

that the hole I shoveled in
will destroy a world of fox

I wonder if ink
will return to stone
I worry that my dog will walk
through glass or step on a bee
I wonder if we'll still remember
how to write our names

I worry about the van
parked at the liquor store
that the hardware store will close
I worry about tar
in the bodies of cormorants
that China has lined our
coffee mugs with lead
I worry that class
will follow us everywhere

I worry this cloud might be
permanent, that a sunspot
will reach out like a tongue
and pull us in

I wish marijuana would bring visions
to the Democratic party
I hope the basement isn't filled with radon
I hope Dick Cheney is convicted of war crimes
I don't think God created polyester
I worry water is unaffordable
I hope we're not too tired
to cross the border

I worry these drugs
are just experimental
I worry the window can't be opened
I hope the tunnel doesn't collapse
while I'm beneath the East River

I think we all
need a vacation
I wish that I were an ocean-
ographer like my father
or the one he could have been
I wish that time could be
turned off like a machine
I hope eventually
we can speak freely
of everything

I'd like to graduate
from the united states of plastic
I'd like to face the future
as if it were a person
I'd like to touch it
and still come home for dinner
I want to introduce you to my boat
I think that everything
can't wait till tomorrow
I hope you're awake
when I get there, that you'll be
with me at the end

Bulfinch

Letting go, going over
from space into time
The cloud was not inflection
it was passage, I misread
the apple, I came back
but the door was shut

The prize for a lion
was not a crown
it was a scar, for beauty
an orange, for coming home
coming home, for good
behavior it was nothing

Life so far had not
been rehearsed, just
another language of
exchange, all it can do
is lie in a word
waiting for a mouth

Alabama

for Maria Ragland Davis (1959–2010)

What you are or could be
What you carry or care for

The sample, the given
The collection, the control

Does it ring, is it ringing
true or false

What you felt didn't matter
to the world outside

The cell, the molecule
Its history, locatable systems

Gun stuck to handle
handle stuck to gun

See the smoke pouring out of
the future, the building

Temper this viewpoint
with obsidian or glass

Kill the light that was burning
through the middle of the screen

What is your position
in the room, at the table

The scene crackles open
who you are or could be

It gasps at the blouse
as the air becomes solid

Paper covers anger
Rock covers flesh

Someone will say something
evil is crazy

Someone will always say
it was nothing

Someone will take
all you are or could be

as a given, as proof of
a mistake in the landscape

Someone tries to drain
all the color from the room

In the end, as the ending
of a given or proof

what you are or carried
can't be covered, will be found

Watertown Is Ninety-nine Percent Land

When I point to the island I mean a body on a map.
Think about the heart: it doesn't have to form a sen-
tence. If the story feels cold it's because the beginning
is so far away. Every city has its battles. One thing lead-
ing to another. A brother's voice can carry out a mission
like a hand. This is where the sound turns pale when I
stop to eat my breakfast. Something gathered in a sack
outside the kitchen is how I feel. Pray for us singers in
the forest of our discontent. All those empty lawns are
staring down the partly cloudy stars. The man in the
boat is trying to plug a hole made of all he'll never have.
Someday even this will disappear into another death,
an absence you didn't know was holding up the future.
Follow the line till it no longer asks for more. Desire is
irreducible, particular. Its name is Georgia. Syracuse.
Cheyenne.

Oil and Water

In the painting was an ocean, as in the voice a history.

What was the woman picking up as she turned?

I filled the bathtub with water. I stocked up on wood. I thought about the spark that sets the oil on fire, the fire that turns the water into steam.

It was more like sailing than sleeping. An eye adjusting to the dark.

A picture giving up its face.

Paper. Scissors. Water.

This is what the work is like.

A story climbs the stairs until its shoes will never dry, until there is no way to descend.

If you were sleeping in the doorway. If you had lain down in the tunnel. If your feet were wrapped in plastic.

If you saw the water like a green, unpeopled train.

If you heard the clatter of a canefield.

This dirty blue, this travertine. This almost-snow.

Dear Kamau.

Dear Michelle.

Dear Lorenzo of Texas and of Vietnam.

It's impossible to say what will last until it's gone.

Dear Paul of the elaborate Russian dream.

I've been trying to catch your eye, but you're too busy
kicking out the sun.

On film, the tower was an interruption. The axis of a
shadow.

A hole into which another world was pouring.

Dear mother of intention. Dear face in the clouds.

Dear Shelley of poetry.

I watched you watch the screen.

Dear Lorca, you are king of the forest.

Your forest a dream made of air.

Dear city of defenses.

Dear Emma of anarchy.

Dear David on the pier.

Dear Barbara of the Genji.

Dear John.

Dear shipwrecked George.

Dear auburn water of the basement.

I tried to call you.

Dear girl in the bakery, you should be in school.

The shore is curatorial.

A drawing erased without the bitterness of friendship, without the gesture of a dare.

The symbol of disaster is mechanical: a fan, a reactor, a bomb.

It is not, as in a watercolor by Hiroshige, a hand composed of water reaching toward you as you run.

In the ocean is a painting, as in the page a voice.

To those who don't know we are drowning, the ocean has nothing to say.

Self-portrait with Imaginary Brother

after Willem de Kooning

Eventually the "imaginary brother"
becomes a wife or a lover, a daughter
or a wife. A "Woman Sitting" (1943)
is sitting in the middle of a war.
The breast that is showing
does not appear to be loved.
It lives in a society of thieves:
no hands. Even the pink lady
isn't pink, she's a head full of teeth. Now
it's 1948. Painters may not be trembling,
but the world is. Turned over,
the secretary is a piece of furniture,
her paint running upward
impossibly from the face. She'll do
anything you say.

Defoe

To have
or nothing
No penchant
no tiger
no boat

The hand
a mechanism
of pulleys
The ear
a hammer
in the head

Slowed down
into a series
of beats
its poet
is dead
almost
simultaneously

Overlooked
by night lights
in a mind
of parking lots
it may be hot
a long time

I wanted it
to go somewhere
else, for a drive
in the country
I belong to
the exhausted air
at the top
of the hill

What is
a petal
Alex
but an edge
at the end
of its moment
I don't want to break
anything
into lines
temporarily

I want to fly
between the garden
and the rose
the scissors
and the water
the water
and the mouth

Steady Digression to a Fixed Point

for Rose Hobart, for Joseph Cornell

A rose can't change the world. It can only open or close.

A rose drives the world like an enormous gear.

It pushes a schooner east of Borneo.

When a body has been rearranged, it is held together with a rose.

A rose is a weapon, a guide, a compass.

It shatters the glass to explain a spilled blue shore. This is how we know we are in the presence of tragedy.

You shouldn't have. You couldn't have. You did. You are.

We piece together an aftermath.

"You" is how we talk to ourselves. "We" is an I that sees itself among others. An assemblage makes of I a "we."

An assemblage is a body for which there is no escape.

A bear, a fish, a chance wheeling in the dark.

A man lifts the girl into a box. By what magic is she sawn in half only for the artist to reassemble her before our eyes?

The body is a formal constraint. It has this one life with which to make eternity.

Form, the form of art, is an effigy of ourselves.

Unlace it. Belate it. Rose it up.

I'm writing your name in a garden, in a box.

Everything in the past, everything in the background, is precarious. The tenement, the jungle, the luxuriously carved wall.

A rose disarms the face of its enemy. Even a bejeweled prince succumbs to this flowering.

In *Rose* the landscape has been all but erased to show an internal topography.

Rose worried. Rose accepting a drink. Rose holding the monkey like a baby.

Rose accepting a man's arm. Rose in a dress vaguely suggestive of bondage. Rose in a suit and tie.

Rose looking inward rather than forward to feel what she will do. Rose struggling with her own reflection. Rose dressed for escape.

Rose fiddling with the tablecloth like a girl who married up.

Rose pleading with the sun.

Rose sleeping in her boots. This is the image with which the prince falls in love, the prince in a glittery gown.

The bed is on a stage, the most public of islands.

Rose is in danger, but her voice can't be heard over the music.

New York is getting fainter and farther away.

She is up all night. She is disappearing.

The C, the O, of the eclipse.

When Rose steps away from the jungle, she is not in a party, she is trying to organize the stars.

Of what state is Rose the enemy?

They cannot pull the names from her mouth.

Oh, un-American beauty rose.

Throw the line into the air and climb until there's nothing.

There is no witness to a rose-colored future.

In the sacred disorder of the box, a rosary. It's not telling us how to think about the hour of our death. It's making a hole large enough to draw a thread through. Long enough to pull a woman back out of the labyrinth.

We were trying to have a conversation. I was trying to write down every word you say. Now I've burned my toast.

Rose Hobart is how he gave you his love.

This is a poem about the death of roses. A film that arose from a rose.

An I looking at the Orient from the edge of a different ocean. A poem about Queens.

We are on the river, East of Borneo. We are east of an island, as Queens is east of Manhattan.

We are in the valley of the stars.

This is Rose out of sequence. Rose on the ledge. A knife in a garden.

The cut at the end of the take. The scene. The reel. The movie.

This is a movie about The End. Of Colonialism.

A rose may blow from Liverpool to New Orleans, from California to Kalimantan. Worked. Worshipped. Grafted. Shipped.

This is the end of exploration. The well-dressed wife coming to salvage the explorer from his native informants.

This is a film about a movie. A movie revolving around a star.

The sun is our star. It is the star of *Rose Hobart*.

We are watching the death of the Sun, a star disappearing, the bulb burning out. A body buried alive in a film, in a can.

The End is behind a curtain, it is in her purse, it is rising to the surface.

The cinema is going dark, snapping shut.

This is a movie about silence. About speaking with your eyes. The heart racing as she strides across the room.

A poem about a volcano, a film about the interior.

What is drawn in the drawing room. What is assembled in the basement. What is taken apart on the table.

The making of a body through a series of omissions.

The violence of the studio system. The California sun. The snowy taupe of the cathode light of Hollywood as seen on TV.

This is a poem about the star system and its ancient astronomer. About a poet of the outer boroughs, looking up. An image thrown into the sky like a searchlight.

This is a poem about a fox. An alligator. The misplaced animals of the backlot.

This is a poem about searching for light behind the deep purple gel of the jungle. A poem about the deep.

The stars resting above the longest night of the year. The winter palace. The rose palace.

This is a passage about being caught in the thatchwork outside the gate. Like a wolf.

About looking into the face of desire until it blinks.

Dear Paolo. I dreamed I would write this. I dreamed a rose was coming out of my mouth in the middle of the greatest city in the world. I dreamed the image of a rose opened in the Museum. It turned in its box like a girl buried alive.

Rose moves inside this blue light. She's coming down. She's skating on a shiny disk. She's walking upside down across the surface of your lens.

Dear Rose, I always wanted to be a star projected onto a blinding white screen. I wanted to be found like a volcanic island. To carry myself through the California air as if I lived in the filtered light of an imaginary jungle. To feel the prickly glitter of the thin lamé gown I was given to walk through the moonlight.

In the middle of the scene, Rose draws apart the curtain and crosses a threshold. She crosses the river from object to subject.

The artist points to her, as to a silent archive of events.

She is going to become the film's only word.

He is moving her body from his eye to yours.

He is saying this film is also a mirror, as all desire is a kind of mirror.

He is saying "I too remain silent." "I rest my case."

Now we are one another.

In the darkroom. In the blink of an eye. In the moment we wrestle by the water.

Leap over the fence, Rose. Jump the cut.

This is not a film about the death of cinema, it's a poem about eternal life.

She is not a bombshell. She is not a volcano.

She's a pearl. A drop of milk. An atom bomb.

The present is full of sound. Time presses against us from every side. The tomb holds a body whose sound has been turned off, a box where pictures are kept.

The mind is drifting down a river like there's something to fish for. But the river is just this.

When the light is turned on, you will forget you ever saw me. All of this will disappear.

The spongy silence around the body of Rose Hobart will fill the room with an occasion beyond words.

Ladies. And Gentleman. I give you. Rose. Hobart.

Suez (1938)

Little Annabella's pretty mouth
is in the sand

A fire in the corner
written by Disraeli

"De Lesscps, Ferdinand!"
scrolling up the stairs

De Lesseps backing up
yet again from the buffet

Who can say
what he desires?

The countess trades her penmanship
for next season's hat

De Lesseps is on the map again
his helmet full of tears

So the future is this ditch:
a scar across the screen

What came first
he thinks

Annabella or her mouth?
genius or monarchy?

The gemmed trouble
of someone else's power

stopping traffic
in love with its own nothing

Coup

Mallarmé's gambling
astonished everyone
even the poets

An acre of paper
sold down a river
whose blackbirds
would only
fly backwards

To abolish
a missing passage

The "never"
of printlessness
shipwrecked within
the greater blues
of untrackable changes

A fight thrown
across a border
unmaintained
as the spyware of the future
in which we used to live

Sonnet 63½

Against love's battle lies: ungrammatical.
Inevitable meadow. A future tensed of all its past.

So time may take this beauty down
but beauty will fight itself to death.

The vampire day, top-heavy, white.
Erase, erased, erasing.

Aggrieved belief. He was my east and west.
He bound my breasts, I cut his hair.

I lay my words upon his mouth,
my mouth upon I cannot say.

All of grace is not device. Love
loves its past but not its thief.

May all its punishments remain untamed
upon this green unsentencing.

Alive

Fear isn't always obvious, but obviousness is one of my greatest fears. If I look like I'm going to faint I hope someone will bring me a paper bag.

A self isn't always self-evident.

Out of the darkened chaos of this thought comes Gertrude Stein. Roast beef. Nickel. Glitter. Difference. Objects objecting. An animated world upcycled into poetry.

I'd like to drink until this is obvious. I'd like to have another life without having to write it down.

I hold some truths to be obvious enough not to have to say them at all.

Even if we both love Swinburne, we're more likely to talk about conceptualism.

I might say something like: "I think there's a kind of conceptualism that makes a joke of the obvious but doesn't allow for the joke to be on the artist, and the absence of that risk makes it boring, the artist wanting to feel smarter than the art, as if she's the boss and it's just the muscle."

That's what my father would call a can of worms.

Which in the language of symbol means a lot of mortality.

I don't remember the moment when it became obvious that my own body was meat, and apart from meat, mostly gristle and bone, and very little of me actually produces words, although it feels compelled to speak for the part of me that *is* dumb meat, which is not dumb at all, only speechless, and not entirely speechless, but needing a translator like Wittgenstein's lion.

I think it was the book about the plane that went down in the Andes. I think it was called *Alive!*, which seems eerily optimistic for a book about cannibalism.

I hate to repeat myself. But I repeat myself all the time.

Embarazada means pregnant, which may or may not be obvious.

People think God is obvious, or not: everything or nothing. A hole held open by a word.

So low you can't get under it.

I admire de Kooning, but I don't love him.

I prefer *Gilligan's Island* to *Survivor*.

I want to read more, but when I think about reading one word after another, it's almost a kind of torment.

Is it obvious that to put out a fire you have to suffocate it?

Sensation is almost as slippery as a word. The darkness of the space where things were.

Obviously whatever I'm composing is decomposing at the same time.

When someone says "obviously," sometimes they're really saying you wouldn't understand.

Obviously I want you to agree with me.

The "family romance" isn't obvious. And then it is.

Not all histories are written.

A dream might not be obvious until you tell someone about it, and then it's all too obvious.

"In a land far away" means I probably won't see the movie or even read the book.

When did western expansion become obvious?

Slaughter sounds obvious but is almost always hidden by a well-dressed figure of speech.

When I saw "blank verse" translated as "white verse," I started writing prose.

Does anyone know what "soft power" is?

When a mystery is made obvious people call it a revelation. But it was there all along, neither uncovered nor covered up.

It was a long time before I realized that William Carlos Williams could have inherited the monogrammed bathrobe of Walt Whitman without anyone noticing.

New Jersey isn't obvious, it's elsewhere.

The letter W is both more and less than a vowel.

When someone in Circulation said they were weeding the library, I thought they said "reading" and I wondered how they planned to do it.

Metaphor carries something across, but from then on, it's fugitive.

A fig leaf only makes a crotch more obvious.

On the radio, I heard someone talk about storytelling as the basis of civilization, as if that were obvious.

It sounded like what they meant was "believe me, I'm important."

If I had to carry such a creature across a river, I would stop in the middle and say "this time I'll be the fox and you be the goose."

It takes someone i mportant to say what they think is obvious and make it sound like they just thought it up.

Who would disagree with that, *you freak?*

Believe me, I couldn't narrate my way out of a paper bag, in case that's not obvious.

I sometimes leave the last few pages of a novel unread.

I used to think it was obvious that I was different but not obvious what that difference was.

Breathing only becomes obvious when you try to hide it.

A tautology seems obvious, but like a rose, it is not.

The difference between writing and painting is not always obvious.

A blue light on the skin may be orange in the eye of the beholder.

Obviousness is 9/10s of the law.

Most people don't know that Golda Meir grew up in Milwaukee. Or that when her mother wanted her to marry she ran away to Denver. Or that she toured the U.S. dressed as the Statue of Liberty in a fundraising campaign for a Marxist-Zionist youth movement.

Abraham Lincoln was in it too. So it looked like freedom meant choosing your own hat.

After her death, Golda Meir was played by Anne Bancroft, Judy Davis, Ingrid Bergman, and Valerie Harper. Not everyone remembers the woman who played Mary Tyler Moore's best friend Rhoda in the imaginary Minneapolis of the 1970s.

Even in imaginary Minneapolis, she wore a headscarf that made her look like she might leave at any moment for a kibbutz.

If we could see what roles we are performing, would we have more faith in them?

Rhoda was the one without anorexia. Imagine her being played by Golda Meir.

In 1975 Putnam published Golda's *My Life*, which was not yet the title of an experimental poem. The title frightens me because I wonder what happens when you finish it. The afterlife?

Even if something's miserable, you might not want it to end.

The expression "Golda's shoes" means, among other things, "really, you're wearing *that*?"

My life in Wisconsin was another story, which did not become a motion picture or a book with a frightening title.

Fifty years after Golda wore the spiky crown of Liberty, I played the witch in a third grade production of *Hansel & Gretel*.

I didn't realize it then but my grandfather was dying, and my witchcraft couldn't save him any more than it could procure me a meal made of imaginary children.

Gretel and I were both in love with Hansel. Why would I want to eat them both?

No one seems to talk about cannibalism anymore.

Apparently children make very good soldiers, it has to do with what they are and are not afraid of. Afraid of adult disapproval, unafraid of eliminating other people to win the attention of a surrogate parent. Unafraid of weapons shaped like toys.

I didn't feel responsible for my grandfather's death. But if it happened now, if I were performing as a witch in a play, if I were playing someone who intends to fatten up a child and eat it like a goose, I might worry. I might picture some child's model of string theory in which my actions in one location caused results in another. It might take me years to get it off my chest.

The last time I spoke with my father he told me about a month he spent in New York the fall before I was born. He was there to get a work visa before he flew to Libya. I was stuck at my grandparents' in Wyoming, within my mother's embarrassment, stamping my annoying little foot against her eighteen-hour girdle.

My father went to see *My Fair Lady* and *Aida*. He walked from the Cloisters to the Staten Island Ferry. He took a boat more than once to an offshore monument, what was it called. It was a very tall woman.

When he was checking out of his hotel and heading to the airport, he loaded all his bags into a taxi, then went inside to pay the bill.

He caught up with the car a few blocks away, as if they were in a movie.

He said, "On the whole, I've been lucky." Which is true, given the various schemes he's been pitched by people he thought of as his friends.

When I was a child, there was not always money to buy meat or eyeglasses or winter boots. We did not live in an opera or a fable. No one was being buried alive exactly, no one would be discovered, the war had been lost, the crumbs went in a circle. I could walk for years in someone else's shoes, making an imaginary fortune with my thoughts. We were all "beside ourselves," as if our lines were being whispered from above.

What makes a person lucky is not always obvious because it's so close to disaster.

I wish I were more famous.

I wish I slept better.

I wish I could take a nap in the middle of the day.

I wish my mother had been a difficult celebrity mother who could be the subject of my international bestseller.

I think that's all for now, we'll be in touch.

Because my grandfather was dying, my mother missed my best performance. We played three nights in a row, each one better than the last. The applause went on and on. It was my new favorite sound.

All this happened one March.

I was never told what my grandfather died of. It sounded like a stomach ache but was probably the same cancer for which he had traveled to Minnesota to receive cobalt treatments, which sounds prettier than it is.

Cobalt is the word I think of when I see Joseph Cornell's Medici prince. It's the color of a body seen through a glass darkly.

When Paul was blinded by God and fell off his horse and said "now we see through a glass darkly but then face to face," *then* sounded like the past, but apparently he meant the future.

The face exists in the future, after you wake up.

Simone Weil thought mercy was a law of ascending scales, an equal and opposite force to gravity. She thought that gravity kept us from being devoured by God.

What's next isn't obvious.

The writing on the wall is too big to see. It's monumental, it's forgetful. A molecule with half a life, then half a life again. Like cobalt, collapsing. Approaching. Rearranged.

See that woman in the harbor, her sandals full of seaweed? She knows she's going under.

She has a question. She's raising her hand.

About the Author

About her: the air, warm as fact.

An imaginary boat heading off to hell, her foot
pushing it offshore.

The sunlit bank, a mirage of the perfect past.

She was barking at the waves, thinking they
barked first.

But this was not a river. It was Thursday, a word
cast in lead.

Her eye had turned the water into sky.

The poet is a trespasser.

The poet is the king of Rome, New York, with
one foot in a boat and one against the snowy
shore of reason.

Wondering if, like a boy, she could go there for a
season.

Notes

SECOND LAW

John Bunyan (1628–1688) was an irrepressible preacher and inveterate swearer, often imprisoned for his defiance of authority; James Hutton (1726–1797), a geologist, physician, meteorologist, and experimental farmer whose observations of erosion and metamorphosis defied the biblical narrative of earthly genesis.

One conceived of the world as a geography of spiritual trial; the other saw it as a dynamic, endlessly revised composition.

Both studied the relation between visible and invisible forces. Both have a place in the history of nonconformity and dissent. Both understood themselves to be part of an immeasurable, unfinished story. Neither of them wanted to shut up.

Their intensive inquiries into space and time resulted in, among other things, Bunyan's proto-novel *The Pilgrim's Progress* and Hutton's revolutionary *Theory of the Earth*.

Bunyan's pilgrim must survive the Hill of Difficulty, the Slough of Despond, the Mountain Vainglorious, and other clearly marked trials in order to reach the river that separates this overwhelmingly legible world from the incomprehensible next life.

Hutton's concept of deep time was grounded in a vision of the earth as an evolving composite organism, within which every landscape was alive. His theory was popularized by John Playfair, a real person who only sounds like one of Bunyan's characters.

According to the second law of thermodynamics, any discrete system shifts toward equilibrium and entropy. It wants to arrive. It wants to come to rest.

The title is borrowed from William Blake. A "Song of Experience."

SONGS FOR A.

Saint Augustine confessed his coming-of-age as a coming into language. His turn toward God was inseparable from his investigation of the space, mystery, and transformative power of words; the way they could be transferred to and contained by the mind; the evidence they provided that the mind could contain things larger than itself.

Augustine of Hippo was a church father who asked to be freed from sin—"but not yet." An African in Rome who refused to see good and evil as black and white. Who wrote an unfinished tale of being undone by an idea. Who saw fallability as a path toward God.

In the looping thought and asymmetrical metaphors of his digressive *Confessions*, he ventured a poetics. You don't ascend but fall toward the divine. You don't take the straight path, you turn.

TURNERESQUE

Against the picturesque landscapes of his time, J. M. W. Turner (1775–1851) placed the unstable picture field of the sea. He turned over the sublime.

Robert Edward "Ted" Turner III (b. 1938), the unlikely, contradictory, and unpredictable entrepreneur of cable television, made an expanded film canon available to wider audiences by subscription. He also tried to make classic cinema more popular by colorizing it—a less successful idea—but I think he understood something about cinema's relation to other versions of the sublime.

A view that seems to approach its viewer, to meet her in between: I think of this as turneresque.

The poems in *Meteoric Flowers* were written in the context of various stories unfolding in the early years of the twenty-first century: among them the "events of September 11th" and the United States' subsequent launching of wars in Iraq and Afghanistan, the increased surveillance of private space, the explicit use of racial and ethnic profiling, and renewed threats on civil liberties related to gender and sexual preference. I would not say that these events are the subject of this book, but they were inseparable from my thinking about codes, pronouns, boundaries, and the ways that metaphors both reveal and hide meanings.

These poems also have in mind, and draw support from, other poets, living and dead. Among them William Carlos Williams, who found and made the news in poetry, and Walt Whitman, who said America was, or could be, a poem. Some of these poems were also written in conversation with a group of friends and poets on the east coast of San Francisco Bay.

Erasmus Darwin, the Enlightenment polymath from whom I borrowed the titles of these poems, was a primary inspiration. Especially his *Botanic Garden* where his scientific research took the form of a long two-part poem complicated by extensive footnotes, conversational interludes, and errata. Darwin treats all components of the natural world not as objects subdued by human intervention but as subjects in their own right. Plant reproduction is presented as a wildly polyamorous world. Humans are likewise treated as part of nature, not as its de facto government, and their violence reverberates against the entire network of species relation. Darwin's poems address everything from gender patterns to the evils of slavery, Franklin's experiments with electricity, the conquest of Mexico, and the relation of poetry to painting. Poetry, Darwin seems to suggest, can be at once an account of the physical world, a rethinking of the order of things, a caprice, and a call to arms.

ALL THE PAINTINGS OF GIORGIONE

Giorgione (a.k.a. Giorgio Barbarelli Zorzo da Castelfranco) is widely considered a major painter of the Italian Renaissance, though he died in his early thirties and precisely what is and is not his work remains open to debate. His canvases are unsigned, and only six surviving paintings are definitively known to be his, though a much larger body of work has been attributed to him. Many of his paintings are known only by descriptive listings in private inventories. Some of them survive only as copies—or presumed copies—of missing originals.

OIL AND WATER

Written for *Oh Sandy! A Remembrance*, an exhibition and event organized by *The Brooklyn Rail* in 2013 around a group of artists who lost work the previous year in the hurricane that flooded much of Manhattan.

WATERTOWN IS NINETY-NINE PERCENT LAND

After the Boston bombing in April 2013, Dzhokhar and Tamerlan Tsarnaev, the primary suspects, were chased to Watertown, where Dzhokhar was eventually discovered hiding in a boat parked in a driveway.

SELF-PORTRAIT WITH IMAGINARY BROTHER

The following are compositions by Willem de Kooning: *Self-Portrait with Imaginary Brother* (c. 1938), *Woman Sitting* (1943), *Pink Lady* (1944), and *Secretary* (1958). He spoke on the subject of "trembling" in a talk delivered February 18, 1949.

In November 2012 I participated in a celebration of Joseph Cornell's film work at the Museum of the Moving Image in Queens, New York. This poem served, in part, as an introduction to Cornell's film *Rose Hobart*, and the following note served as an introduction to the poem:

When I first saw Joseph Cornell's nineteen-minute film *Rose Hobart*, I thought it was one of his late works, that it had been made twenty or thirty years after *East of Borneo* (1931), the primary source of its footage. But *Rose Hobart* was first shown in 1936, when most of its images were only five years old. Cornell's film was not a tribute to the Past; it was the rearrangement of a recent passage. He had turned a dull movie into a brilliant screen test, a false geography into a silent portrait.

Like a ship, it took the name of a woman.

East of Borneo—in which Rose Hobart sails from London to the South Seas in search of her husband—was released the year of Cornell's first dated collage, in which a carefully cut rose is pasted onto the rigging of a schooner.

In Cornell's first exhibition at the Julien Levy Gallery, this collage was exhibited with another, in which a woman is being sewn together by a machine whose driving mechanism is a flower. She appears to be both two- and three-dimensional, a corn maiden, a mannequin, a paper doll.

In another work of the same year: a severed hand under a bell jar, a rose in the center of its palm, and an eye at the center of the rose. Roses were under observation.

Joseph Cornell was born in 1903; Rose Hobart, two and a half years later. She grew up in Manhattan and Woodstock. He grew up in Nyack and Queens.

She began as a stage actress and was appalled at the working conditions when she arrived in Hollywood. In her autobiography, *A Steady Digression to a Fixed Point*, she writes that when *East of Borneo* was being filmed, she was so physically wasted, she had to stuff her evening gown in order to keep it from falling off.

She began working for the Screen Actors Guild, organized other actors, and fought for an eight-hour workday.

For this show of insolence she was summoned to appear before the House Un-American Activities Committee in 1949. Ronald Reagan, the new head of the Screen Actors Guild, and many others chose to speak. Rose Hobart chose to remain silent except to defend the right to remain silent.

She was blacklisted and her career in film was over.

SUEZ (1938)

Concerning the film adaptation of a colonial occasion directed by Allan Dwan, starring Tyrone Power as Ferdinand de Lesseps (who engineered the Suez Canal), Loretta Young as Countess Eugenie, and Annabella as the French-Egyptian woman with whom both Power and de Lesseps fall in love.

SONNET 63½

A loose translation of Shakespeare's sonnets 63 and 64.

ALIVE

"Alive" was written for a live performance at Apexart in New York in March 2013.

ABOUT THE AUTHOR

"Only those who do not know how to think what they feel obey grammar. People who want to control their own expression use grammar. The story is told about Sigismund, King of Rome, that he made a grammatical error in one of his public speeches and responded to the person who pointed it out to him in this way: 'I am King of Rome and am above grammar.' And the story goes on to say that from then on he was known as Sigismund 'super-grammaticam.' A wonderful symbol! Every person who knows how to say what he talks about is in his way King of Rome. The title isn't bad, and its soul is being oneself." (Fernando Pessoa, *The Book of Disquiet*, translated by Alfred MacAdam)

Acknowledgments

My thanks to the editors of the journals and anthologies in which many of this volume's new and uncollected poems first appeared: *A Public Space*, *The American Reader*, *Colorado Review*, *Company*, *Critical Quarterly*, *Dusie*, *Epiphany*, *Everyday Genius*, *Jupiter 88*, *The New Yorker*, *Poetry*, *For One Boston*, *Oh Sandy!: A Remembrance*, and *The Sonnets: Translating and Rewriting Shakespeare*.

Deep gratitude to Suzanna Tamminen and to Wesleyan University Press for publishing *Meteoric Flowers* and *Address*; to Rosmarie and Keith Waldrop of Burning Deck for publishing *Turneresque*; to Stephen Ratcliffe of Avenue B for publishing *Second Law*; to Ann Lauterbach for selecting *The Human Abstract* for the National Poetry Series and Dawn Drzal and Paul Slovak of Penguin for seeing it into print; and to Rachel Levitsky of Belladonna for publishing an earlier draft of "All the Paintings of Giorgione" as a chapbook.

Thanks to the Guggenheim Foundation for its generous support; to PEN/New England; to the Ucross Foundation; to Patty Willis and Mary Lou Prince; to Shonni Silverberg and John Shapiro; to Ronald and Thora Willis.

I am grateful to Paolo Javier for inviting me to respond to the films of Joseph Cornell; and to Charles Bernstein for the occasion that prompted me to write "Alive" and Albert Mobilio for the venue in which it was first presented.

My thanks to Jen Bervin, Lisa Jarnot, and Elizabeth Savage for their generous comments on this manuscript; to Susan Howe and Robert Creeley for early guidance; to Peter Gizzi for reading poems along the way; and to Lisa Cohen for her astute readings of poems and manuscript drafts.

This work is indebted to the fine company and care of more people than I can say, including many writers, friends, and family in addition to those mentioned above. By way of beginning: thank you, Adrienne, Africa, Alan, Anne, Barbara, Ben, Bill, Brenda, Bruce, Bruni, C. A., Cecile, Cecilia, Cliff, Dana, David, Eleni, Fred, Gay, Gayle, Gertrude, Harvey, Jack, James, Jena, Jennifer, Joshua, Julian, Juliana, Kamau, Kent, Kristin, Laynie, Lee Ann, Marjorie, Mark, Matt, Micah, Michael, Michelle, Myung, Nancy, Nate, Norma, Omar, Pam, Pascale, Penelope, Piotr, Richard, Robert, Sarah, Sheila, Simone, Steve, Susan, Thomas, Tonya, Vanessa, Vincent, and Wes.

Thank you, Jeffrey Yang, for your generous spirit and your vision of this book. Thank you, Edwin Frank, Sara Kramer, and New York Review Books.

NAJWAN DARWISH Nothing More to Lose
Translated by Kareem James Abu-Zeid

SAKUTARŌ HAGIWARA Cat Town
Translated by Hiroaki Sato

MIGUEL HERNÁNDEZ *Selected and translated by Don Share*

LOUISE LABÉ Love Sonnets and Elegies
Translated by Richard Sieburth

SILVINA OCAMPO *Selected and translated by Jason Weiss*

A. K. RAMANUJAN The Interior Landscape: Classical
Tamil Love Poems

PIERRE REVERDY *Edited by Mary Ann Caws*

ALEXANDER VVEDENSKY An Invitation for Me to Think
Translated by Eugene Ostashevsky and Matvei Yankelevich

WALT WHITMAN Drum-Taps: The Complete 1865 Edition
Edited by Lawrence Kramer

ELIZABETH WILLIS Alive: New and Selected Poems